WHY

DO WE HAVE TO LISTEN TO PEOPLE WE DISAGREE WITH?

THE COMMON GOOD

MICHAEL SALAKA

PowerKiDS press.

New York

Published in 2019 by The Rosen Publishing Group, Inc.
29 East 21st Street, New York, NY 10010

First Edition

Editor: Jennifer Lombardo
Book Design: Tanya Dellaccio

Photo Credits: Cover Diego Cervo/Shutterstock.com; p. 5 Monkey Business Images/Shutterstock.com; p. 7 Steve Debenport/E+/Getty Images; p. 9 wavebreakmedia/Shutterstock.com; pp. 11, 21 Syda Productions/Shutterstock.com; p. 13 Pressmaster/Shutterstock.com; p. 15 Gagliardilmages/Shutterstock.com; p. 17 Hung Chung Chih/Shutterstock.com; p. 19 Hero Images/Getty Images.

Cataloging-in-Publication Data

Names: Salaka, Michael.
Title: Why do we have to listen to people we disagree with? / Michael Salaka.
Description: New York : PowerKids Press, 2019. | Series: The common good | Includes index.
Identifiers: LCCN ISBN 9781538330883 (pbk.) | ISBN 9781538330876 (library bound) | ISBN 9781538330890 (6 pack)
Subjects: LCSH: Listening–Juvenile literature. | Conflict management–Juvenile literature. | Interpersonal relations–Juvenile literature.
Classification: LCC BF323.L5 S25 2019 | DDC 153.6'8–dc23

Manufactured in the United States of America

CPSIA Compliance Information: Batch CS18PK: For Further Information contact Rosen Publishing, New York, New York at 1-800-237-9932

CONTENTS

Good for Your Community

A community is a group of people who live or work in the same place. Community members often share the same ideas and values. Sometimes, however, they'll disagree. It's not **realistic** to think everyone will agree about everything all the time. It's important to understand that it's OK to disagree. Sometimes it's even helpful.

For communities to run smoothly and members to be happy, people need to work toward the common good. When you work toward the common good, it means you do things that **benefit** everyone in your community. Listening to people you disagree with is one way to contribute, or give, to your community's common good.

It's only natural for people to disagree from time to time. The things people disagree about may be different based on their community. There are many types of communities, and people can belong to more than one at a time. Your neighborhood is a community. Your school and classroom are communities, too.

Disagreements at School

At school, your teacher may sometimes break up your class into groups. You might be asked to work together or choose a team leader. Not everyone in your group may agree on what to do or which person to choose. It's important to listen to the views of the other people in your group.

Even though you may not agree with someone in your group, it shows respect when you take the time to listen to their **opinion**. Disagreements sometimes help people make useful changes. Try to be open to new ideas when you listen to people you disagree with. Someone might have an idea no one else in the group has thought of before.

Everyone in your group should have the chance to share their point of view. After all, everyone has a right to their own opinion. Listening to these opinions, even when you disagree with them, is good for the whole group. If everyone is heard, the members of your group will work better together.

Conflicts and Compromise

Sometimes listening to people you disagree with might cause a fight. This is when people get angry with each other because they have different opinions. When people fight, they aren't working toward the common good. They're working against each other instead of working together. This isn't a good way to get things done.

One good way to solve **conflicts** such as differences in opinion is to compromise. When people compromise, it means each side gives up something they want so they can come to an agreement. When groups compromise, they find a middle ground that all members can agree on. Compromising is working toward the common good.

Be a Good Listener

It's not always easy to listen to people you disagree with. However, you should always show other people respect and be open to hearing their opinions. By being a good listener, you show the people in your community you care about them. Always treat other people how you'd want them to treat you. You can tell them your own opinions when they're done talking.

Be **polite** when listening to people you disagree with. Don't interrupt, or cut them off, when they're talking. Everyone can have their own opinion, and you should respect this right. Also, if you don't listen to what someone's saying, you won't know why they have their opinion and you might not learn new information. When you listen to people you disagree with, you work toward the common good of your community. Everyone should have the chance to be heard.

GLOSSARY

benefit: To be helpful or useful to.

conflict: A fight or strong disagreement.

opinion: What someone thinks about something.

polite: Showing good manners and respect for others.

realistic: Based on what is real or true to life.

INDEX

WEBSITES

Due to the changing nature of Internet links, PowerKids Press has developed an online list of websites related to the subject of this book. This site is updated regularly. Please use this link to access the list: www.powerkidslinks.com/comg/listen